THE SAFE & HAPPY SENIOR DRIVER

How To Drive Through Your Golden Years in Florida and Beyond

By Frank Rapisardi, M.Ed.

TABLE OF CONTENTS

INTRODUCTION

YOU CAN STILL ENJOY DRIVING AS YOU ONCE DID! Well almost! Now from a Senior Driver Safety Consultant with a sense of humor, and God knows you will need it, are my many years working with senior drivers and others on successful driver safety techniques in several states. Now for Florida and other senior states of retirement, a hand book of safe driving practices.

This is my first full book on safe senior driving, besides the multiple presentations and articles I have published for newspapers, magazines and educational groups.

I'm keeping it short on purpose. All you need to do is read it in its entirety first. Then review from time to time the areas that may need attention, as in causing you concern, to keep yourself and others safe. On average, you usually know which ones are problematic for you without a formal assessment.

Use this as a reference book. It's not a coffee table book. As a senior driver myself I recommend you pull it out from time to time and review some specific area of personal concern.

Stay ahead of the curve before something happens. Don't wait for it to happen. As a senior driver, this should be one of your bedside reference books. Short and sweet but with the possible answer to your driving concern that day. Don't laugh. You'll have one.

CHAPTER ONE:
When To Say Uncle

Okay, let's get this one out of the way first. Is there an age you should automatically stop driving? The answer is a BIG FAT NO. Why? Because we are all physically and mentally different. The state of New Hampshire and one other state that shall go unnamed, previously required seniors at age 80 to automatically be road retested. This was not only unconstitutional but age discriminatory. I personally met with the head of the DMV in New Hampshire at the time and did an article for a local newspaper which I felt was instrumental in getting this discriminatory law overturned.

Yes a time will come when you should stop driving. Warning signs will appear. It may be a visual, mental or physical issue. It may be the result of a surgery or a debilitating illness. Act on them.

Let's start by checking your present driving ability here: **http://fitnesstodrive.phhp.ufl.edu/us/**

Anyone can take this assessment. You will need to do this activity with a spouse or close family member or friend who knows you well.

Again, this is just an online assessment of your driving skills and not a clinical assessment. But it's a good starting point. If you feel you have any serious concerns after this assessment, follow the steps in the next paragraph on formal driving assessments.

Also, if for any reason you need to stop driving immediately, search out the different types of alternative transportation available to you in order to continue your life in an effective manner.

If you feel the need for a more formal assessment try these below.

First have a formal road test with a certified driving instructor (driver ed teacher). Take it further if necessary with a formal Driver Rehab Specialist for more serious mental and physical issues. These are highly trained occupational therapists. If you have a grandbaby who can't make up their mind on a college major, point them in this direction: Driver Rehab Specialist. God knows we need more of them.

They will administer a 2-3 hour test, including road test, testing you cognitively and physically. Contact your local hospital for this one.

This time will come for all of us. It is what it is. Accept it and move on. Nothing wrong with getting chauffeured around too, is it? Just think of yourself as one of the Rockefellers now and you earned every bit of it.

CHAPTER TWO:
Things You Must Do To Stay
A Fit Driver Physically

Now that we got that one out of the way, let's start some safe driving.

Act like you ARE still alive. Act like driving has a significant purpose. Get off your duff and do things that will especially help your driving in the long run. Also do ones that remind you how important it is to keep driving safely for as long as you can. Like what for example you say? Okay, here are a few suggestions. First let's work on your personal physical fitness. Remember to check these activities out with your doctor first if you have any concerns, even the smallest one.

Aging constantly changes us physically. When driving, we need certain physical skills such as good vision, hearing, mobility, leg strength, flexibility, coordination, etc. Decline in some of these is gradual, especially hearing, but some are more rapid. In addition medications we take that affect our driving, as well as physical impairments or illnesses, need to be dealt with, not put on the shelf. Let's get started.

1. Walk, even for a few minutes daily. It costs nothing and may show some of your cute neighbors that you'd like to meet that you are training for the local Senior Olympics. Especially if you carry light weights and

pump some iron while walking. It will also show those obnoxious neighbors that you can still chase their dog off your lawn.

2. Get a light object and use it as a weight to strengthen both arms and hands. Be careful to not let it slip out near your spouse. Oops.

3. Get your eyes and hearing checked annually. Ninety five percent of driving is visual. If you keep saying "What?" to your partner, turn up your hearing aid or get a new one. You'll have more friends, too.

4. Don't miss your annual physical checkups. Hey, usually Uncle Sam will pay for it at our age anyway.

5. Do foot and leg strengthening exercises that you check out with your doctor first. Push a light object (not your husband or wife please) with your foot, one leg at a time. Increase the resistance gradually. Remember if you get that hernia you can't drive at all and you'll have to listen to your sister-in-law or brother-in-law babble on and on while driving you around.

6. Ask your senior center to bring in experts on senior mobility, flexibility, and leg and arm strengthening exercises for driving to help lead a workout program.

7. Eye hand coordination activities are great for senior drivers. Play this one with a partner. Take a ruler with the one inch mark on the top. Have a partner drop the ruler straight down between your two open hands. See how quickly you can catch it with both hands (at what number on the ruler). Keep trying to lower the number indicating your response time is improving.

You will find a whole list of physical activities to improve your driving in your free copy of my copyrighted publication ACT below.

CHAPTER THREE:
Assessing Yourself And Your Driving Skills

My late Italian grandfather, Nano, a quiet man had several verbal gems of wisdom that he would depart with when we grandchildren were driving him crazy with noise. One frequently used one, when we repeatedly disobeyed one of his requests was "What are you a stunadoo?" Gently translated in English, "What don't you understand about what I said, dummy?" Ouch!

Okay, I get it now. If you are doing something wrong with your driving that needs correction, and you repeatedly hear it from others, do something about it immediately. It's called self assessment and its accompanying correction. Seniors MUST constantly assess their driving skills and make corrections where necessary. If you wait and keep putting it off, someday it may be too late. As a senior driver you must constantly self assess your driving skills and make corrections in order to remain a safe driver. Usually these are just minor corrections like coming to a full stop at a stop sign, looking down the road in all directions better or using your turn signals properly. Don't be a "Stunadoo". Assess yourself from time to time. You usually know your areas of weakness from repeated spouse comments anyway. See, they really do have a purpose. Just kidding! You'll find more in the included ACT supplement.

1. Start with your doctor. Tell him/her about your driving habits. Ask about your medications and their effects on your driving. Ask him/her for his recommendations. Doctors are required by the *AMA* to discuss driving with you. They are busy so make it for a future appointment. Don't be a pushy noodge.

2. Have an annual vision and hearing test. Ninety-five percent of driving is visual. Vision tests will usually require insurance or out of pocket cost. But here's my gift to you: a free hearing test

http://www.ascentaudiologylakewood.com/hearingtest for Floridians and others. Scroll up to the Online Hearing Test. See what you are missing without a computer? Don't tell the rest of the world but anyone can get this free test there too.

3. Take advantage of some of the free offerings from the included ACT supplement to self-assess yourself. Print your scores out and date them so you can keep track of your progress.

4. Take a safe driver senior driver course from *AARP* or *AAA*. They are good for three years so you must review what you learned from time to time in their textbook. Many insurance companies will even give you an annual auto insurance discount for taking the course. In Florida it is the law. This is one of the reasons for this book; to help you review any previous instruction you may have had and build on it with additional safe driving ideas. You don't wait three years for the next class like some knuckleheads do.

5. Attend a free *Car-Fit* session where you and your vehicle will get a FREE checkup. Bet you never heard of it. No driving is involved. So don't panic, you can't fail and there is no test. They will help fit you properly to your vehicle to be a safer driver. They will also give you and your vehicle a free checkup. Florida has an outstanding program. One of the best in the country. I know. I'm one of their certified technicians. Find information in the ACT supplement. Best thing since sliced bread.

6. Discuss your driving with a close and adjusted friend or relative (not WACKO cousin Bob). Have them go for a ride with you to observe you. Have them take notes on anything they observe that is possibly needing correction for your driving safety. Don't be thin skinned. It's only meant to help you. Discuss it when you get home privately.

7. If you feel you have some serious driving issues, start out with an evaluation by a licensed driver education teacher. It may only be minor and correctible. If not, they will point you in the direction of a more formal driving evaluation performed by an occupational therapist. They are usually found at your local hospital by appointment. The occupational evaluations are expensive and usually not covered by insurance. Don't be cheap. If you have to, and need it, and can afford it, do it. Some of the VA Hospitals offer this service for free.

No one likes to have their driving skills criticized. But it's not criticism , think of it as constructive suggestions to make you an even better and safer driver than your pompous neighbor who is always trying to top you by bragging how much better a driver they are than you. We all have one.

CHAPTER FOUR:
Safe Driving Requires Good Mental Stability

This is your second major area of concern: THE STATE OF YOUR MENTAL HEALTH.

Thinking skills are crucial to safe driving and include items such as reaction time, decision making speed, attention, information processing, impulse control, memory and mental flexibility. Wow! Some seniors will want to take a nap now just after reading that list, never mind working on them. Don't panic. If you are an average, healthy and adjusted for the most part senior, you will only need to concern yourself with a couple of them, unique to you and your driving habits and skills level. Usually you don't have to be an expert to know what area needs work. That's why self assessing is so important. Here is an explanation of each mental skills area to help you decide which ones need work for you. Suggestions on how to improve each thinking skill can be found in my included ACT supplement.

I'll put the key ones in layman's terms.

1. Reaction time: How long does it take you to react to something you see or hear (even feel) while driving? Driving is obviously very sensual. Don't get excited you lovers out there, I didn't mean it that way!

How quick are your responses when driving? If you need to swerve, brake, or accelerate out of danger can you do it quickly enough? This is one of the easier ones that you can work on and improve. There are multiple activities you can do with your computer to improve reaction time. If you are constantly blaming the other drivers for everything, you are probably the one at fault and need correction. Accept it and do something about it.

2. Decision making speed : This is simply how fast you can make the correct decision when driving. Correct being the key word here. To avoid a pothole, should you swerve left or right? To stop in time to avoid a pedestrian or animal? Reading traffic signage quickly and correctly enough to drive safely is essential.

By now all you wizards out there have figured out this is similar to reaction time. Almost. Except here you have to make the right decision. It's reaction time plus choosing the correct action while driving. Depending on your age and physical health, this area of decision making can be crucial for you to assess correctly. Get help if you feel you have a serious issue with this skill. You may need to cease your driving if you no longer can make safe decisions and quickly enough.

For the average senior, there are tons of activities online that will develop how fast and accurately you can make these decisions. Date the activities you use to develop a faster speed and keep track of your progress. Don't worry, no one is perfect and you will probably still screw up from time to time but you can lower the number of wrong choices from where you were before with practice.

3. Attention level: The level of attention you exercise when driving.

One of my favorite sections of this book. Why you ask? Because I keep asking myself do I really have to even explain this one? Let's see. Have you ever brushed your teeth while driving? Combed your hair? Put on makeup? Read a book? Ate a hamburger? Dropped a lit object onto the seat? Got dressed at 40 miles per hour? Checked out the cute neighbor next door? Of course you have. But if you are still doing it, you are a distracted driver. You are an accident waiting to happen and need an immediate correction. There are multiple online activities and books that you can use to practice improving your attention level. Do it today.

4. Information processing: How well and quickly do you process road signage and directional postings and make the appropriate decisions.

The rate of speed that you accomplish this varies from individual to individual. No two seniors are alike. There are online games and activities you can practice to increase the speed that you process visual and auditory stimuli. This is a crucial skill you can't ignore.

5. Memory: As we age our memory skills tend to lose a little to a lot of their edge. Have you found yourself forgetting directions lately? Can't find your glasses? Walked into a room and you forgot what you came in for? I think my wife hides my glasses to get even. Seriously, memory is very important to driving. It comes into play every day. But there is hope for the average senior unless you have an organic issue needing medical attention. Here are some suggestions with more in the ACT supplement below.

• Look for television game shows like *Jeopardy* that require you to use your memory. Not *Let's Make a Deal.* That will only raise your entertainment level. Make your own scoreboard. See if you can raise your scores. Keep track and date them. Always date your practices to measure improvement.

• Play some brain games on the computer. Again, go to the library if you don't have one. There are private games you pay for and free ones from sources like *AARP* and *AAA* to develop memory. I love the free ones being the cheap curundjon that I am. They work just as well for your needs.

• *The University of Florida* found certain video games such as Medal of Honor improve driving skills. Grab a grandchild and hold on.

• Try to learn a new skill or hobby that is challenging.

• Switch your dominant hand. Try to do tasks using the hand you don't normally use.

• Reflect occasionally on how driving has changed over the years and what is needed to be a safe driver today. Discuss it with others.

• Plan your driving route ahead of time. Know exactly how you are going to get somewhere.

Yes you can improve your driving memory and thinking skills if you work at them. In other words, the more you challenge your brain, it has even been found scientifically that you can increase the number of your brain cells. Nice.

CHAPTER FIVE:
Common Sense Doesn't Cost Anything

This was one of my mother's favorite lines. Not only was she beautiful but brilliant as well. She was so talented there wasn't anything she couldn't do: sew, cook, design her own clothing, etc., so I figured I had better listen to her. Yet the one thing she was always hesitant to do was drive a car. Go figure.

Driving isn't rocket science. You push the accelerator to go, the brake to stop. But there are a few other things in between aren't there? Think of some of the idiots you know who do it and do it successfully. Sounds simple enough, right? But why do some people have a difficult time doing it safely and successfully? It's because the world as we know it and those in it have changed. Including YOU. In this section I want to talk to you about using your biggest asset: age and maturity.

Let's talk now about using that common sense you were born with and developed over the years to be a safer senior driver. After all, with age comes wisdom right? So there is at least one area where you still hold an advantage. Use it. Here are some common sense tips to make you that safer driver.

1. Don't wear those side blocking glasses or sunglasses. Our peripheral vision is already reduced

with age and they only make you look like a scuba diver out of water. Ouch!

2. Don't take off your hearing aid. Do it later at home if you need to look cool. Besides, if you block that oncoming emergency vehicle you can get fined and no one our age likes to spend money unnecessarily.

3. Get all the freebies you can. Ask your senior center to bring in speakers on senior mobility. Hold some free workout classes to improve your flexibility, mobility and leg strength.

4. Practice improving your visual attention rate of speed which prevents focusing too long on one thing such as lane changes etc. while neglecting rear traffic and many other things.

5. As muscles lose strength turning the steering wheel may get harder for some even with power steering. Don't drive wide on turns.

6. Try to learn a new skill or hobby that is challenging.

7. Physical exercise and sports with emphasis on eye-hand coordination can help you cognitively. You are never too old to beat your in-laws at ping pong. Try learning a new sport or physical activity like dancing. Tango anyone? You'll find many more of these common sense senior driving suggestions in the ACT supplement below.

CHAPTER SIX:
Automobiles, Roads, And Even You Are Changing

Just one more thing for us old timers to worry about you say. Hey it isn't anything you can't deal with if you try. We are the product of The Greatest Generation aren't we so we come from pretty good stock and our kids will be even smarter than we are as seniors. By the way, leave this book to them in your will and tell them where they can get more copies of it kind people. My grandchildren's children will need the royalties to pay their college loans. Driving and cars will be here for awhile, don't worry. *The Jetsons* are still a ways off.

Let's start with the automobile.

We are at the beginning of the self driving automobile revolution. You may not be aware but states are already designing and building their interstate systems around this concept. Roads are being built, at times more narrow, in order to implant signaling devices to monitor traffic numbers as well as equipment to control traffic flow and communication between vehicles.

Automobiles are already communicating with each other and roads. These systems, V2V, V2X, V2N, etc. relate to the automobile and its relationship to everything from other cars, pedestrians, driverless cars, and roads and bridges that change their direction based on traffic flow. This will be even more critical to driver safety as time goes by. It will be used for everything from controlling traffic flow to accident prevention. Even changing the shape of your vehicle to fit its parking space. Maybe they can turn mine into that Ferrari I always wanted. Don't panic. It's still a ways away.

Road surfaces are changing and now are being built out of multiple materials as well, probably for future added electronics. Everything from plastic to recycled garbage. These new surfaces will eventually affect your driving. The Japanese and the Germans seem to have the edge on durable road surfaces. The Germans mix rock with their traditional asphalt and are very successful with paving longevity. The Japanese are experimenting with everything from rubber to plastic and successfully.

Limestone, low friction blacktop in Denmark, salty compounds called bischofites in Chile, rubber, and even garbage. These roads will all be self repairing as well to save costs.

With the changes already appearing from global warming, road surfaces must change. Los Angeles is already painting their roads white to diffuse heat.

States and even countries will need to communicate with each other in regards to traffic flow. Your trip from the States to Mexico or Canada may soon be connected and monitored by sensors placed in strategic areas.

Automobiles are now being designed with these future options in mind. We have come a long way since that first Ford Model T. The car of the future is here now. If you can, try to read up on some of this future automobile engineering and road design. You don't have to be a gear head or rocket scientist either. It will only benefit you in the long run. Knowing where you are going with automotive technology and the surfaces you are driving on can only help you get there safer.

CHAPTER SEVEN:
Let's Talk You And Only You

This is where I get personal now. No, I'm not going to ask you your weight or your waist size. Instead let's personalize a long term driving program just for you. Is it possible to individualize a driving program for a senior you ask? Yes it is up to a point. Then the rest in terms of how you carry it out, is up to you. Let's get started.

1. Let's begin with what are your driving needs and priorities. First establish these individualized priorities. Doctor's visits, food and necessities shopping, socialization events, exercise programs, hobbies, volunteering, seeing the grandbabies, and just being an overall positive contributor to society. As stated earlier, if you drive with a purpose, your safe driving will be more meaningful to you and others. So start a mental list now.

2. Can you set up a schedule, for the most part, that you can stick to? It doesn't have to be a strictly rigid one, but one that gives you some order and discipline to your driving. Leave a free block of time for unexpected but necessary trips. That way you can only be but a more determined and successful driver to get there and safely. You have now maximized the value of your driving.

3. Plan your trips better. Combine them so you only have to go out once. The less trips you make, the less chance of you having an accident caused by a careless driver. Plus you'll save gas.

4. Plan your driving route ahead of time. Know EXACTLY how you are going to get there. I mean EXACTLY.

5. Try to travel with a friend. An extra set of eyes and ears never hurts when driving. Just don't pick someone who turns out to be a major distraction and doesn't ever stop yapping.

6. Do a mini car checkup every time you get into your car. Walk around it looking for any liquid leaks underneath or badly adjusted side mirrors. Keep your lights' lenses and mirrors clean. Make sure your seat is properly adjusted for you before starting up.

7. How about this one? Start a senior safe driver support group? Why not? Everyone else has one. You can organize it from your senior center. Develop a network of friends you can count on if you have any car issues, mechanical or otherwise. Share safety tips, reliable and honest repair facilities and route directions to hard to find locations. Members can also point you in the right direction for car repairs with trusted garages. Bring in free automotive speakers on different auto related subjects including the local police. They'll knock each other over getting to you especially the retail ones. Share tips on everything from repairs to inexpensive gas stations. There is a support group for everything. Why not senior drivers?

8. The more you personalize your driving the more you will be invested in it. Don't be afraid to initiate activities with others that help reinforce this concept.

9. Buy the correct car for you. Easier opening doors and better visibility should be a priority. Bring someone with you who may know a bit about cars to help you with your next car purchase. Fit your next car to you. Try adjusting the seating position so it fits you to a tee. If the salesperson won't take the time to explain everything, and I mean everything, go somewhere else.

10. Here is a great website

http://www.aarp.org/auto/driver-safety/

for you to personalize your senior driving skills even more.

CHAPTER EIGHT:
Driving And The Law For Seniors

You say is this section really necessary? I haven't received a ticket in over forty years. Well, probably true but it doesn't mean that you haven't committed a violation or two without even knowing it. You just haven't been caught. So how do you avoid a situation like that? Education.

Here in Florida, where there are many senior drivers, you will need to enroll in a senior safe driver course and/or go online to get the book with all the state motor vehicle laws. Now the state of Florida no longer passes out free driver's manuals unless you are a person studying for your driver's license. Ugh. Well they have to cut the costs of state government somewhere, right? But if you use a computer, you can find the entire driver's licensing book

http://www.flhsmv.gov/resources/handbooks-manuals/

with all the rules online. Read it in its entirety. Have your spouse test you on some of it.

Why is it necessary to stay up with your state's motor vehicle laws you ask? First so none of your neighbors will roll over laughing at you because you were just fined $100 and points on your license for making an illegal turn right in front of Patrolman O'Brien.

Secondly, because your traffic violation could cause injury to yourself or others.

I'm going to discuss some of the important traffic laws for the state of Florida in this section. Why you say? Probably because we have so many senior drivers here now, especially in season who are violating them one after another. Plus if you come down, you'll have a head start on avoiding a ticket. Good? Good!

Here are some of the more important ones. I won't put down all the money fines. You can look them up while paying your bail money. Just kidding.

1. Florida law prohibits using a false name or making a false statement with up to a $500 fine.

2. Florida law requires all drivers and front seat passengers to wear a seat belt. Passengers under age 18 must be belted.

3. Texting is now illegal when driving and or using a cell phone while in a school zone.

4. Driving while impaired will result in heavy fines with possible loss of license.

5. U-Turn lanes: This is a good one to know future Floridians. You can make a u-turn in a designated left lane. Read the arrows carefully. Just only do it there and make it as quickly as you can safely looking to your front, left and behind you. Floridians tend to be impatient waiting for people reversing their direction.

6. Bicycle Lanes: These are increasing exponentially here in Florida. Take them seriously. Bicyclists can come out of those lanes to turn or avoid obstacles.

7. Crosswalks: More prevalent than ever in busy areas. Most are now lighted with automatic flashing stop

lights. Deaths and serious injuries have occurred from careless drivers. Don't be one.

8. Traffic Sign Shapes and Colors: Know your traffic sign shapes and colors before you start driving. Do you know the difference between a crossbuck railroad crossing sign and a no turn on red sign? Not sure? No turn left or right on red. You must wait for the green signal.

9. Left lane must turn. If you goof up, make the left turn and carefully reverse your direction.

10. Reduction of lanes: Left line is straight, right line is squiggly. The lanes will reduce.

11. Divided Highway ends: Triangular shape, two arrows going in opposite directions. Divided highway will end in 350 ft. to 500 ft.

12. Blue and white service signs: Especially important if you are new to Florida. These are for gas, food. motels and hospitals.

13. The state of Florida is presently going through a rotary or roundabout revolution. Due to abundant funding from the federal government, they are being built everywhere to increase and ease traffic flow and safety. Even year rounder Floridians are still not use to them. Use caution.

14. Pulling a trailer in Florida: Rear two reflectors, one at each side with a brake light if the trailer blocks the brake lights on the towing vehicle.

15. Red Arrow: I get this one all the time in my driver ed classes, even from long time year round Floridians. Do not make the movement shown by the arrow until the green light appears. After stopping, you may turn right if there is not a NO TURN ON RED sign and the

way is clear. Key word "clear" cowboys and cowgirls. ALWAYS yield the right of way for any pedestrian no matter what.

16. School Zones: We cherish our children and grandbabies here in Florida. School signs will warn you. At the school crossing, slow down to posted speeds, watch for children and crossing guards. Stop if necessary. When you enter a school zone a reduced speed will be posted. Police in Florida monitor these religiously and you will be fined.

School bus laws are standard as in many states. Flashing lights means slow down and get ready to stop. Come to a complete stop when Stop Sign emerges with red lights flashing on bus. Observe for children entering or exiting the bus in all directions. You may not proceed forward until the bus Stop Sign is withdrawn and its flashing yellow lights are extinguished. If you are on a divided road by a five foot barrier of grass or concrete, you are not required to stop. But still execute caution.

17. Florida Speed Limits: You are NOT allowed to drive ten mph over the speed limit. That is a myth everywhere, including Florida. You can also be fined for driving too slowly blocking or delaying traffic. Keep up with the legal speed limit flow and you should be fine. Highways with 70 mph speed limits also have 50 mph as their minimum speed. Below that speed will get you a ticket.

18. Making Turns: You must use vehicle turn signals or hand signals (from the vehicle's left side) when turning.

19. Passing on the Right: Is only legal when there are two or more lanes of traffic moving in the same

direction or the vehicle you are passing is making a left turn.

20. Rain, Fog and Smoke: If rain, fog or smoke appear, head lights and windshield wipers must be activated.

21. Flashing Emergency Lights: This is a no-no in Florida. It is against the law to use them in a moving vehicle. That's right, a no-no. Sorry, but that's the law. Take it up with the judge.

22. Power Outages: We've been known to have a few here in Florida. When traffic lights go out, treat an intersection as a four way stop. Be careful getting across the intersection. Very careful.

23. Your Responsibility After A Crash: If you are involved in a crash that results in damage to property, injury, or death, it is your duty - required by law - to give information and render aid.

24. Hit and Run Driving: Leaving the scene of an accident will get you your first felony. You don't want to visit our Florida jails on your vacation now do you?

25. Automobile Insurance Laws In Florida: Florida law requires drivers and vehicle owners to maintain insurance to cover costs in case of a crash. These laws include the No-Fault Law and Financial Responsibility Law. Check with your insurance agent in your home state *asap* if you are going to remain in Florida as to what you need to do if not permanently moving here. You must be insured in the state after 90 consecutive days. Always carry proof of your registration here in Florida or elsewhere as well as your proof of insurance card for that vehicle as well as your present driver's license.

CHAPTER NINE:
You Have The Ability And Skills To Be A Safe Driver For Many Years to Come

Easier said than done you say. If you are a realist like myself and you seriously work at your personal driving areas needing refinement in this senior driver's manual, yes you can keep driving safely for many more years. Look, by now at our age you know nothing comes easily, right? Anything worth doing is worth the effort. Driving is one of the most important senior functions we need to hold onto. It gets you to your doctor, out to socialize, helps maintain your good mental health, gets you to sporting, recreational and educational events , assists you with your necessary life functions, gets you to work, gets you to the arts, and keeps that daily independence you have earned and deserve. No senior wants to lose that for as long as they can. IT'S YOUR INDEPENDENCE AND MOBILITY AT STAKE! Keep it for as long as you can safely.

I have laid out the key senior driving points to continue to be a successful driver. The rest is up to you. If you are moving to Florida or any other state for your retirement, this book is essential for you as a reference book. All of the senior driving techniques apply anywhere. Just apply them in your new state of residence with their laws and driving requirements.

Let's do a quick review of the key elements of safe senior driving in Florida beginning with the need for you to be invested in your driving ; translated, how much do you want to keep driving for as long as you can and safely? Do you realize and understand how important it is for you to maintain your independence? Nothing is free. It takes work to be a safe and effective senior driver in Florida with the increasing number of drivers but it is more than do able and essential for your well being.

You can be a safe driver for years to come but you must work at it. Then when you no longer have the necessary physical and mental skills to be a safe driver anymore, you need to put your keys away and seek alternative transportation.

Remember there is NO MAGIC AGE for a senior when this time will come. Don't wait till it happens. The smart senior will plan ahead to stay mobile. This is why the need for continual self assessment is necessary. Like other of life's events, it comes to all of us when least expected.

So how do I maximize my safe driving years? Work at your physical and mental skills. Constantly self evaluate. Make your driving purposeful.

Knowing how you are doing as a senior driver will help extend your years behind the wheel. The more you are aware of your abilities, the safer and longer will your driving years be. Constantly assess yourself and make any necessary corrections for safety. You owe it to others.

Much of driving is also a mental function. The sharper you are the better a driver you will be as a senior. Just look at some of your senior friends who are good drivers. Stay sharp through utilizing mental activities that develop your mental acuity. Don't be a mental couch potato.

Also add to your mental driving capability with the use of good common sense. It doesn't cost anything. By our age you should have tons of it. Well most of us anyway. I'm sure we all pulled some stupid driving errors when younger. But now you use your maturity to be a wiser and safer driver.

To end up the driving journey that you took in this book with me, I always like to pass on this quick personal story of my own youthful driving indiscretion back in the day. This episode from my youth probably brought me to eventually be the safe senior driver consultant I am today.

Years ago I was going up to visit a new girl friend, Debby Reynolds, with a fellow teenage buddy. I had borrowed my older sister's new car to see Debby. Yes, that really was her name and she was as cute as the real one.

Driving home on a back, darkly lit secondary road in New Hampshire, the road ended at a T intersection and I, not paying attention to the lack of lighting, drove her car into a curb totally destroying the front suspension because I forgot to put the high beams on.

Fortunately no one was hurt but my sister didn't speak to me for months. And Debby and I split up shortly after. That was my one and only lack of common sense driving experience. Ever.

Fortunately it just involved my vehicle and no one was hurt. Don't know if cracking up her car was worse or Debby breaking up with me shortly thereafter when I was a teenager. Probably Debby.

There. That's my youthful lack of common sense story. What's yours? We all have one so don't be embarrassed. That was then. This is now. Maturity is now your golden ally.

Remember, as a mature senior driver now, any driving indiscretions you may have had are hopefully all behind you, replaced with good, solid maturity and common sense. You must continue always being that responsible senior driver you are now. With a little work, you can be.

Don't forget that your driving skills as a senior are always evolving. Stay on top of them. You paid your dues on the learning curve but must keep learning. Your road is now wide open for you to drive safely for as long as possible. Good luck!

ACT:
ASSESS, CHOOSE, THINK

Let's "ACT" to Drive Longer and More Safely

Presented by Frank Rapisardi, M.ED.
Senior Driver Safety Consultant
"The Automobile Helper"

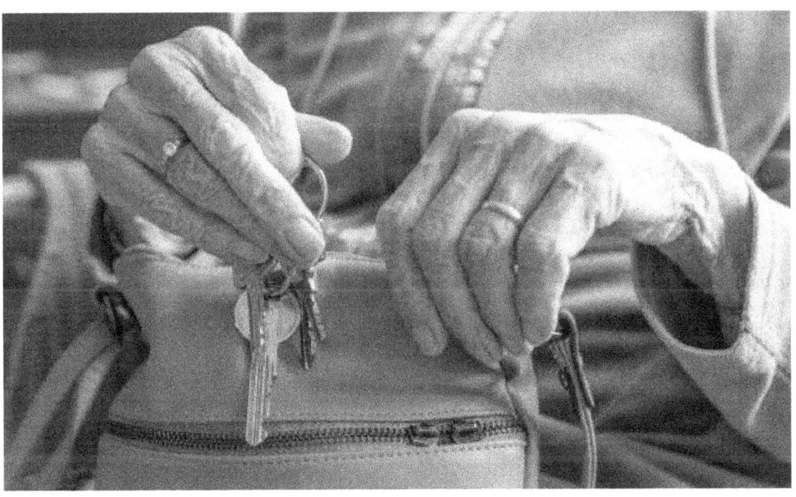

Copyright ©2010 Frank Rapisardi
BONUS ADDENDUM

FIRST ACT:
ASSESSMENTS

1. Begin assessing your driving skills with your doctor. First, inform your doctor of your driving habits. Then, ask if your overall physical and mental condition is safe for driving. Ask the doctor about the medications you take and their possible effect on your driving. Inquire if the doctor has any recommendations for you to stay a safe driver, including possible adaptive devices to assist you in driving safely if you have any physical impairments.

2. Have an annual eye exam. Ninety percent of driving is visual. After age 55, eyesight changes dramatically. Less light comes into our eyes, affecting how we see objects. Have your depth perception, peripheral vision, and visual acuity checked. Test for glaucoma, cataracts, and macular degeneration.

3. Take a FREE and formal hearing test from time to time. Hearing loss is so gradual that you might not be aware of it. Many major business chains such as *CVS* and *Sears* hold free annual hearing tests at their stores. Get a free hearing test:

http://www.ascentaudiologylakewood.com/hearingtest

4. If you use a computer, take a FREE *AAA Roadside* Review test online:

http://www.seniordriving.aaa.com

Even if you aren't computer savvy, have someone at the library or Senior Center show you how. Then, throw a Senior Driver Assessment Party at your local senior center or library, or take it privately at home. Click on the self-rating tool and click on Driver65Plus to test yourself.

Take the FREE 65+ Self-rating form from *AAA* from time to time:

http://www.seniordriving.aaa.com

Keep them in a folder to see your progress.

5. Send for FREE assessment booklets, available to senior centers from both *The Hartford Insurance Company* online:

http://www.thehartford.com/lifetime

and from *AAA* (phone number is in back of *AAA* pamphlets), or online (click on "products", then "free"):

http://www.aaafoundation.org

Check times and dates to take an *AARP* or *AAA* senior safe driver course online or in person:

http://www.AARP.driversafety.org

http://www.seniordriving.aaa.com

You can also attend a FREE *Car-Fit* session:

http://www.car-fit.org

in your area. Offered by *AAA*, there is no driving involved. You park your car and trained technicians will evaluate your driving position as to position of the airbag, visibility over the dash, your proper use of controls, proper seat belt usage, proper use of pedals, your flexibility, etc. They will offer suggestions to improve your position and make you a safer driver. There are Occupational Therapists there who will advise you on the use of adaptive driving devices if necessary — all free!

6. Discuss your driving with a close (and well-adjusted) family member or friend. Possibly have them go for a ride with you from time to time and observe your driving, taking notes on both strengths and weaknesses. You'll find a great list of things for them to observe in today's handout booklet, 'When You Are Concerned'. Don't discuss anything until you return home. Be open to constructive criticism. They are doing this to help you, not criticize you.

7. If you use a computer, take the Drive Sharp Now senior driver assessment:

http://www.drivesharpnow.com

8. If you feel you have some serious driving issues after some of these assessments, go for a more formal driving assessment. Have a licensed driver's education teacher who has experience with senior drivers evaluate your driving.

9. Take a formal driving evaluation one level higher (especially if you have recently suffered some type of debilitating illness). Seek a more in-depth and formal evaluation from either *ADED* (Association for Driver Rehabilitation Specialists):

http://www.aded.net

(or call toll-free 1-866-672-9466),

Or try OTA (American Occupational Therapist Association):

http://www.aota.org

(or call 301-652-2682).

These two organizations provide specially trained occupation therapists who will perform both a clinical test and a road test. They will give you a more intensive and clinical (hospital-like) evaluation. They will suggest adaptive equipment and techniques if needed. Evaluations of this type cost between $200.00 to $600.00. Some insurances will cover part or all. Some VA hospitals offer them for free.

10. Talk to your local Veterans Administration to see if they offer any formal driving assessments.

NEXT ACT:
CHOOSE A PLAN

Now that you have assessed your present driving skills, CHOOSE an appropriate remedial plan of action. Set up a weekly schedule and stick to it. Here are some simple suggestions if your driving skills need improvement. Remember, they won't improve unless you review and practice developing them. **However, if your driving skills are severely impaired, you should seek out professional help such as a Driver Rehabilitation Specialist or Occupational Therapist as previously mentioned.**

COGNITIVE ISSUES: Thinking skills are crucial to safe driving and include items such as reaction time, decision making speed, attention, information processing, impulse control, memory, and mental flexibility, just to name a few. Usually, you don't have to be an expert to know what you need to work on after taking your assessment. But if you are still uncertain, many of these cognitive areas are explained fully with helpful suggestions to improve them in the previously mentioned *AAA Roadside* Review assessment online.

HELPFUL TIPS FOR COGNITIVE ISSUES: Try alternating these activities until you have tried them all.

1. Set up a weekly schedule to play some brain games on the computer that develop memory, information

processing, attention, decision making, and your useful field of view when driving. *Drive Sharp* computer games, produced with *The Hartford Insurance Company*, have lowered senior driver's crash risk by 50%. Go to *DriveSharp*:

http://www.DriveSharp.com

PositScience:

http://www.PositScience.com

and *Neuronation*:

http://www.Neuronation.com

to find brain games online. Several of them have free games.

2. Play a video game with the grandkids! That's right! The University of Florida found certain games such as *Medal of Honor* improved driving skills and visual attention in older drivers. Plus, you'll be a big hit with the kiddos!

3. Try to learn a new skill or hobby that is challenging.

4. Look for television game shows that require you to use your memory quickly, like *Jeopardy*.

5. Try using your non-dominant hand. Use the hand you don't usually use to perform everyday tasks.

6. Every three years, take an *AARP* or *AAA* Driver Refresher Class and freshen your cognitive skills.

7. Retake the *AAA* Roadwise Review Assessment frequently and try to better your score in the cognitive skills section.

8. Play a reaction-time game. Here's a simple one: You will need a partner. Have a partner hold a ruler pointing down in the air over your open, extended writing hand. Have your partner drop the ruler between your fingers and see what number you can catch it.

9.Handle driving distractions by identifying the four different types (visual, auditory, physical, and cognitive) ahead of time and have a plan to deal with them.

10. Plan your driving route ahead of time. Know exactly how you are going to get somewhere.

11. Get a free state driver's manual from the DMV online and memorize the section a the back with the road signs, signal, and markings. Have a partner test you on them.

12. Here's a really good one: Play the "How Should I Prevent It?" game. Have a partner make up a dangerous situation that could occur while driving. Using a stopwatch, see how long it takes for you to present a safe solution to prevent it. Write down your times and repeat the same questions with one new one but in a different order a week later and time yourself again. Try to lower your times.

13. Physical exercise and sports with emphasis on eye-hand coordination can help you cognitively. Try learning a new sport or activity.

14. Reflect occasionally on how driving has changed over the years and what is needed to be a safe driver today.

15. Finally, get your sleep. You'll be sharper with your thinking skills and avoid being a drowsy driver.

PHYSICAL ISSUES: Aging constantly changes us physically. When driving, we need certain physical skills such as good vision, hearing, mobility, leg strength, flexibility, coordination, etc. Decline in some of these is gradual, especially hearing, but some are rapid. In addition, medications we take that affect our driving, as well as physical impairments or illnesses, need to be dealt with, not put on a shelf.

HELPFUL TIPS FOR PHYSICAL ISSUES: Practice 3-4 different ones per week

1. Don't wear side-blocking glasses or sunglasses when driving. Our peripheral vision is already reduced with age.

2. Wear your hearing aid while driving. Minimize the volume on the radio and passenger conversation. Still having hearing issues? There are devices that can be installed which will flash a visual signal to you in place of an auditory one.

3. Ask your senior center to bring in an expert on senior mobility, flexibility, and leg strengthening exercises for driving to help lead a workout program.

4. Play more eye-hand coordination sports.

5. Take an *AAA* or *AARP* Safe Driver class to learn more exercises necessary for safe driving.

6. Do at least 15 minutes of exercise a day.

7. See an Occupational Therapist about adaptive devices such as pedal extensions, spinners, wide angle mirrors, ease of exit/entry tools, etc. to help you physically improve your driving beyond your present adaptive devices. Contact the *National Mobility Equipment Dealers Association* at 1-800-833-0427 for qualified dealers and installers.

8. Wear the correct lenses and put them on before you start out driving.

9. Practice scanning techniques learned in *AAA* and *AARP* Driver Safety program classes.

10. Improve your visual attention rate of speed which prevents focusing too long on lane changes while neglecting rear traffic. *AAA Roadside* is great for this.

11. Look into special glasses that reduce glare and have a telescopic function.

12. Here's a simple pre-driving exercise to help check mirrors and prevent fatigue: Touch chin on chest, tilt head backwards until forehead is parallel with ceiling.

13. As muscles lose strength, turning the wheel gets harder- don't drive wide on turns. Use the power steering and/or a turning knob (spinner).

14. For improving reaction time, use your learned distance and scanning rules more, especially ahead while anticipating danger.

15. Help see better- keep glasses, mirror, lights, and windows clean. Make sure mirrors and lights are adjusted properly.

16. Manage your chronic physical conditions better. Seek ways to minimize their effect on your driving. Talk to your doctor or physical therapist.

17. Minimize driving's physical requirements by driving under optimal conditions.

18. Have your driving position checked at a *Car-Fit* event. It will help you to maximize the physical skills necessary for safe driving.

19. Select a vehicle that is "Senior Friendly". Look for those that offer power adjustments, adjustable pedals, large instruments, ease of entrance/exit, larger mirrors that automatically dim for glare, easy to work controls, better visibility, etc. Seek help if you are unable to do this yourself.

20. Leave spaces between you and other drivers to help with reaction time.

21. Note landmarks and exits that will help you navigate and make driving less strenuous, both physically and mentally.

22. Wear appropriate clothing and shoes when driving.

23. Learn more about how your car works. That way, you will be prepared for unusual circumstances that arrive and may affect its physical operation.

24. Avoid left turns unless protected by a green arrow. Make three right turns at the next right instead and you will be on the road you want.

25. Avoid driving at dusk, dawn, night, and any low-light situations.

26. Never drive when tired/drowsy. Always ask your doctor which medications affect your driving and how.

27. At night, adjust your speed to the range of your headlights and look slightly to the right when another car's headlights are too bright.

28. Have a salesman or other automotive professional explain available "Senior Friendly" automobile technology such as "blind spot monitoring systems".

29. Slow down at least 10 miles per hour. Research shows that 90% of older drivers who fail reaction tests at high speeds perform satisfactorily at speeds ten miles per hour slower.

NEXT ACT:
THINK ABOUT YOUR DRIVING

Think more and often about driving to increase focus and awareness.

1. Think about being an AWARE driver, not a COMPLACENT driver.

2. Read frequently about new senior driving techniques and issues.

3. Think about taking a refresher class with *AAA* or *AARP* every three years. Attend a *Car-Fit* Checkup session.

4. Think up a weekly schedule to do cognitive and physical activities to improve your skills.

5. Think about your driving limitations. No one is Superman or Superwoman.

6. Think how driving is a function of ability, not age. Just because you have been driving for 60 years doesn't make you a great driver.

7. Think about your resources. Help is available online, at the DMV, at government agencies on aging, at your doctor's office or hospital, at your senior center, from senior organizations, from your family, from fellow seniors, *AARP*, *AAA*, etc.

8. Think about setting up a "Senior Safe Driver Support Group" at your senior center. Organize a *Car-Fit* Checkup session or *AAA/AARP* Safe Driver class for your

center. Attend a senior driver expo. Hold discussion groups on safe driving. Bring in speakers like local driver education teachers, a doctor or pharmacist to discuss the effects of medication on driving, occupational therapists to talk on adaptive devices, *AAA* driver safety specialists, or the *AARP* Driver Safety Program director in your state.

9. Think about helpful tips from this presentation and review them. Try a new one each week.

10. Think about how a car works. Talk to a knowledgeable person or invite a local automotive repair shop owner or vocational schoolteacher to come in and talk to seniors about the basic workings of a car and the new automotive technology helpful to seniors.

11. Think more about driving and the law. Have the local police talk to seniors about recent changes in the law, the common infractions that occur with seniors, and how to prevent them.

12. Think about the state legislation affecting senior drivers, such as Mature Drivers Vision Test or the restrictions the DMV can impose on your driving.

13. Think about how driving has changed since you first started driving. Talk about what is involved in driving today with others.

14. Think how driving is a privilege, not a right. Think about responsibility to the other drivers and pedestrians that you share the road with by being an Aware Driver.

15. Think about teaching a fellow senior a new age-appropriate driving technique that you learned. Don't do it when either of you are driving, but beforehand and in detail. Ask them to tell you later what happened

when they tried it and discuss it. Be supportive, not critical.

16. Think that an AWARE driver is both a SAFER driver and a LONGER driver, and you will be on your way to a happy driving life!

ABOUT THE AUTHOR

Frank Rapisardi is an award winning educator, writer, automotive journalist and senior driver safety consultant. During his thirty five years in education, he was awarded the inaugural Lloyd Reuss Award, President of General Motors, for teacher excellence in science and math in 1998. Recipient of multiple education awards from Special Education Teacher of the Year to state Nominee for Massachusetts Teacher of the Year award. He holds a Master's Degree and Bachelor of Arts Degree in Education from Massachusetts universities. Developing his educational expertise further, he has written educational curriculum for environmental schools in New England.

Always writing about his second passion, the automobile, during and after teaching, he became a member of multiple automobile clubs and organizations serving as a director. Upon retiring from education, naturally a future with automobiles followed. His greatest love along the way was for the Italian marque, Alfa Romeo, of which he owned several.

Frank is presently a long time professional member of *IMPA*, the highly respected, International Motor Press Association in New York as a Senior Driver Safety Consultant. Acceptance into *IMPA* membership originally was limited to just the highest level of the automotive press community. Recently diversifying its membership further, *IMPA* today includes all aspects of the automotive industry.

He served as the European Editor for *Nissan Sport Magazine* in New Mexico for four years, covering and writing articles on Nissan racing in Europe. He was responsible for interviewing many famous automotive personalities along the way from Rene Dreyfus, French Formula One Champion of the 1930s, to the famous Japanese Mr. K of the Datsun 240Z fame. His writings carried him around the world from California to Monte Carlo. Along the way, as a member of the automotive press, he covered multiple motoring events, writing and reporting events for European readers such as The Pebble Beach Concourse d'Elegance.

In addition he has done several articles and is an authority on famous automobiles and their inventors and development in the North East. He is an authority on the historic Massachusetts electric cars of the early 1900s. It was the carriage industry there begun in Amesbury, Massachusetts that led to Detroit and the American Auto Industry. Henry Ford was said to have based his Detroit automobile assembly line on the Amesbury carriage assembly line.

During this time in New Hampshire and Massachusetts he developed a further interest in the needs of the senior driver. He began volunteering to help seniors in multiple ways: teaching safe driver classes, writing senior driving articles for senior publications and working one to one pro bono with senior drivers. Here he began to take a deep interest in the too often neglected senior driver. Dedicating the last ten years of his life, and himself now a senior, he has focused on developing senior driver well being practices. His wealth of knowledge abounds in this book as he continues striving to make senior drivers safer.

Frank lives in Sarasota, Florida, with his wife Julie and their Havana Brown, Mia.